THE L.I.F.E. CURRICULUM

Living Is For Everyone

KENNETH K. LAW

Unless otherwise indicated all scriptural quotations are taken from the New King James Version.
Boldface type in the Scripture quotations indicates the author's emphasis.

All dictionary definitions are taken from Merriam-Webster.com, 2015, http://www.merriam-webster.com.

THE L.I.F.E. CURRICULUM
LIVING IS FOR EVERYONE

Copyright © 2016 KENNETH K. LAW
All rights reserved.
ISBN-10: 0-9978393-0-9
ISBN-13: 978-0-9978393-02
eBook ISBN: 978-0-9978393-1-9
Printed in the United States of America

Cover by Loman Creative Services

All rights reserved no part of this book may be reproduced or transmitted in any form or by any means, electronic or mechanic-including photocopying, recording or by any information storage and retrieval system-without written permission from the publisher.

Lawken Publishing
P.O. Box 15876
Savannah, GA 31416

L.I.F.E. CHANGING CURRICULUM

Pastor Law has written an amazing, transforming and heart provoking curriculum that is a must have for all Pastors, Ministry Leaders, Marketplace Leaders and for the emerging Leader. Many are gifted in their skill of expertise but fall short in the areas of integrity, character, communication and how to navigate in various systems. Pastor Law's unique God-given ability to operate as a surgeon to go deep into those wounded areas that have been hidden traumas in your life but managed to manifest in all of your personal, ministerial, and business relationships. This is a must read because of the transparency, the love behind it and the successful outcomes that will spawn from reading it. Pastor Law's own personal walk in the role of a Pastor coupled with his own life lessons more than qualifies him to produce this thought provoking curriculum.

I approve and highly endorse this curriculum because it will revolutionize how you lead!

-FIRST LADY LAWANDA RAGIN LAW

DEDICATION

To the Holy Spirit, I dedicate my first work unto You. I give back to You what You first gave me. You gave me a Word and I gave you back a book. Thank You for your inspiration, revelation and encouragement.

TABLE OF CONTENTS

	Acknowledgments	i
	L.I.F.E. –Living is for Everyone!	1
1	FROM MAINTENANCE TO INTENTIONAL LIVING	2
2	THE BIRTHING PROCESS	14
3	OVERCOMING THE JEZEBEL SPIRIT	28
4	THE POWER OF GRACE	42
	SALVATION PRAYER	55
	ABOUT THE AUTHOR	56

ACKNOWLEDGMENTS

I want to thank my beautiful wife, LaWanda, for every sacrifice that she has made for me, the ministry and the Kingdom of God! Thank you so much for loving me and believing in me! Great is your reward!

A big thank you to Cory and Leza Chandler for digging this out of me and dedicating the time and love to this project! You planted the seed that this could be done! You guys are very special to me!

A warm thank you to LaToya Williams for your much needed assistance and dedication to this venture! You're a great daughter!

Thank you to our parents and family who stand with us and pray for us daily! We love you to life!

A special thank you to the church I serve and lead, New Birth Savannah Church! Words cannot describe how much love I have for you all!

A great thank you to my pastor, my friend and my father Bishop Eddie L. Long! I follow you as you follow Christ! I love you very much.

LIVING IS FOR EVERYONE!

As a Pastor I am privileged to cross the paths of people from all walks of life. The people I encounter have various experiences that have framed their outlook on life. Some of those experiences are traumatic and have caused them a great deal of pain. In my observations as a leader in the Body of Christ, I notice many have not yet mastered the ability to overcome trauma. Trauma has forced many into a place of just existing instead of living. God never intended for you just to exist on the Earth. He wants you to experience life and have it in abundance. Jesus came to preach the good news to the poor, heal the brokenhearted and proclaim liberty to those that are held captive (Isaiah 61). Yet, many of God's people are trapped in the cycle of poverty; hearts are broken and are entrapped in mental prisons.

My observations cause me to ponder, "Why are some people living the life God intended and others are not? Did those that are living life as God intended; grow up with a silver spoon in their mouths? For those that are just existing and not living, were they dealt such a bad hand in life they are unable to recover?" God wants all of his people to LIVE no matter the trauma they have experienced in the past.

Living Is For Everyone. God wants you to have a L.I.F.E. during your time on this Earth. It is my prayer that *The L.I.F.E. Curriculum* will provide you with a solid foundation in order for you to begin to pursue *L.I.F.E.* like God intended. God is not a respecter of persons. He will respond to your faith just as anyone else who has tapped into the *L.I.F.E.* He has provided through His Son Jesus Christ. Let's journey through this curriculum together. Grab your bible, a pen and an open heart to receive what God will speak to you throughout this book. It is time to LIVE because *Living Is For Everyone!*

CHAPTER 1

FROM MAINTENANCE TO INTENTIONAL LIVING

Have you ever been driving and out of the blue your check engine light pops up on the display. I don't know about you but there are a few surprises I can live without and the check engine light is definitely one of them. I can remember exactly what stretch of I-20 I was on the last time I had that daunting warning pop up on my display.

Even though I am a man of extreme faith and belief in God, at 9:30pm, my faith was failing me. I began to declare and decree I will make it home without delay. I arrived home and was greeted by my beautiful wife but honestly – it is kind of funny - I can't tell you how I got there because the check engine light distracted my drive. Kenneth Law's New Living Translation: Fix it Jesus cause NOW IS NOT THE TIME TO HAVE TO GET A NEW VEHICLE! Now I don't know what your interpretation is whereever you are from around the world reading this but you get my point!

Let me dive a little deeper into this thing. Fast forward: I go to the dealership to have them take a look at things and all of a sudden it hits me like a ton of bricks. **Perhaps like many of you, while I had been so busy doing the work of the Kingdom, as it related to my vehicle, I had gone into maintenance mode – going intothe dealership only for routine oil changes and tire** rotations instead of being in an intentional mode where I was thinking ahead and anticipating the needs of my vehicle before the light came on! I hope you feel me and hear the kingdom revelation coming out of my spirit right now.

> **In the Spiritual realm maintenance is not enough.**

Let's go a little further. There is no question that it is important to engage in maintenance – the care or up keep; support; the action of upholding or keeping in proper state or being - especially of a vehicle. However, what if I were to tell you that in the spirit realm "maintenance" is not enough! What if I told you that you could engage in maintenance all the way to hell? What if I were to tell you that our greatest enemy of God's intentional and pre-ordained purposes in our lives is a maintenance mindset?

I see you reading with that questioning tone and saying, "Prove it Kenneth". Follow with me as I pull this matter out using four points to ponder below. See, *the way I see it*, before we can understand this matter we must first ask the question, why maintenance alone can produce spiritual blockers in the lives of believers?

Below are some things to ponder:

Ponder Point #1
God never called us to just maintain and/or sustain. Think about it! All throughout the Bible, God tells us one thing in a variety of ways. The Bible says in Genesis 1:28, "Then God blessed them and said, Be fruitful and multiply. Fill the earth and govern it. Reign over the fish in the sea, the birds in the sky, and all the animals that scurry along the ground."

Ponder Point #2
When we just maintain, all we do is keep in existence or continuance; preserve; retain. A maintenance mindset blocks change!

Ponder Point #3
When we engage in a maintenance mindset, all we do is keep it in an appropriate condition or operation. We don't enhance it; we just keep fixing it.

Ponder Point #4
A maintenance mindset is a fixed and debilitated position; which keeps something in a specified state and/or position.

I see that I've captured your attention a little bit but let me go a little further. Maintenance also means, "to practice habitually" and "hold in the hand". So if we are habitually practicing and/or rehearsing something, all it means is that we can train our brains to do the same thing over and over and over and over again without any change. We know that to do something OVER AND OVER WITHOUT ANY CHANGE IS INSANITY!!!!!

Now that I have peaked your interest, I want you to take a moment and write down a few ways in which your life has been in maintenance mode.

_____

_____

_____

_____

_____

_____

_____

_____

List a few practical things you can do to overcome the spirit of maintenance.

1._____

2._____

3._____

PROPHETIC DECLARATION

<u>Before the end of this lesson, I declare there is going to be a supernatural release of kingdom dominance and authority in your life as the Lord reveals and heals the areas of your life that have been limited by a maintenance mindset and propels you into the intentional living of the Kingdom of God. In Jesus name -Amen.</u>

The Restrictions of a Maintenance Mindset

Albert Einstein once said, "Insanity is doing the same thing over and over again and expecting different results." While I wholeheartedly agree with the great doctor, I think that a maintenance mindset – a pre-established set of behaviors and beliefs that lack innovation, forward moving thinking, and a breaking away from the status quo may be even more detrimental to the body of Christ.

Let's review this familiar New Testament story of the talents as I believe the behavior of one of the servants illuminates my ponder points on the dangers of a maintenance mindset.

Matthew 25:14-30 NKJV; *[14]"For the kingdom of heaven is like a man traveling to a far country, who called his own servants and delivered his goods to them. [15]And to one he gave five talents, to another two, and to another one, to each according to his own ability; and immediately he went on a journey. [16]Then he who had received the five talents went and traded with them, and made another five talents. [17]And likewise he who had received two gained two more also. [18]But he who had received one went and dug in the ground, and hid his lord's money. [19]After a long time the lord of those servants came and settled accounts with them. [20]So he who had received five talents came and brought five other talents, saying, Lord, you delivered to me five talents; look, I have gained five more talents besides them. [21]His lord said to him, Well done, good and faithful servant; you were faithful over a few things, I will make you ruler over many things. Enter into the joy of your lord.' [22]He also who had received two talents came and said, 'Lord, you delivered to me two talents; look, I have gained two more talents besides them. [23]His lord said to him, Well done, good and faithful servant; you* *have been faithful over a few things, I will make you ruler over many things. Enter into the joy of your lord.* ²⁴*Then he who had received the one talent came and said, 'Lord, I knew you to be a hard man, reaping where you have not sown, and gathering where you have not scattered seed.* ²⁵*And I was afraid, and went and hid your talent in the ground. Look, there you have what is yours.* ²⁶*But his lord answered and said to him, 'You wicked and lazy servant, you knew that I reap where I have not sown, and gather where I have not scattered seed.* ²⁷*So you ought to have deposited my money with the bankers, and at my coming I would have received back my own with interest.* ²⁸*Therefore, take the talent from him, and give it to him who has ten talents.* ²⁹*For to everyone who has, more will be given, and he will have abundance; but from him who does not have, even what he has will be taken away.* ³⁰*And cast the unprofitable servant into the outer darkness. There will be weeping and gnashing of teeth."*

There are several points I want to highlight here about the restrictions of a maintenance mindset.

First, I am wholeheartedly convinced that a maintenance mindset will always restrict intentionality. I hear you asking, "What are you saying Pastor?" I am saying that it is my earnest belief that you have to be intentionally committed and committed to be intentional. <u>By intentional, I mean that you have to engage in committed, consistent, and conscious movement towards your Kingdom mandate and assignment with keen focus, skill, agility, direction, and leadership when your assignment is popular and unpopular; when its pleasant and unpleasant, and when its pleasing and unpleasing to yourself and others.</u>

I am convinced that having a "Maintenance Based Mindset" tells God that you don't want to move forward, you don't want to change, and you really don't believe what you prayed.

Let's look at the intentional mindset of Jabez.

> 2 Chronicles 4:10 NKJV: ¹⁰*And Jabez called on the God of Israel saying, "Oh, that You would bless me indeed, and enlarge my territory, that Your hand would be with me, and that You would keep me from evil, that I may not cause pain!" So God granted him what he requested.*

Jabez didn't only want to maintain where he was; he wanted to move beyond where he was and he asked God to do just that. Let me express this a different way. Jabez was **intentional – focused, skilled, and directed** – in his asking from start to finish! He was clear that he wanted more than what he currently had in his hand and he cried out to God specifically and directly for more. As leaders, we must follow the model of Jabez as the results of his intentionality are unquestionable.

Secondly, a maintenance mindset can prohibit positive results. Some people don't see the results they desire because they are not committed to the process that leads to the desired end results. In other words, some people give up too soon because of the unpopular, unpleasant, and unpleasing aspects of their Kingdom assignment and fall back into a posture of maintenance of the status quo as opposed to breaking through to a new threshold of Kingdom possibilities! As Bishop Kenneth Ulmer powerfully proclaimed, "it is painful but it is necessary!"

> **A Maintenance Mindset will always restrict intentionality.**

Finally, a maintenance mindset can create a debilitating mindset. In other words, this type of thinking gives many excuses and justifications for why there is no forward moving progress. Just like the man with one talent, this mindset checks you more than the enemy ever will as it becomes debilitated by the paralysis of over-analysis.

The Teachable Moments of the Third Servant

In reviewing the life of the third servant, there are a few notable teachable moments that we can all learn from. First, the third servant never tried to do anything intentionally. He didn't try to be innovative, creative, or progressive in his thinking. As it is recorded in the book of Matthew, he did ABSOLUTELY NOTHING! Now before we condemn him again, let's take a moment to examine the behavior of the third servant because at one time or another we could all relate to it.

Listen closely, as we look at our *first teachable moment* of the third servant. It seems clear that he had more of an attitude and mindset of "maintaining" what he had instead of "growing" what he had. As a result of his attitude, what he held on to left him anyway. Do you understand what I am saying? Whenever we get to a place where we refuse to let go and grow what God has entrusted to us, even our best efforts of maintenance will become futile as God can't put new wine in old wineskins.

Our *second teachable moment* is so closely tied into teachable moment number one that we may miss it. The truth is that if we can become so preoccupied and focused only on maintaining what we have we can miss enhancement and upgrade opportunities that are all around us. What am I saying? We must be careful not to become so myopic and narrow focused that we miss the growth and expansion that is right up under our nose.

> **We can become so preoccupied and focused on maintaining what we have that we miss enhancement and upgrade opportunities.**

Our third teachable moment is about the dangers of complacency. Complacency is *"the act of pleased, especially with oneself or one's merits, advantages, situation, etc."* Complacency often occurs without an awareness of some of the potential dangers or defects. In my opinion, the third servant's complacency was the greatest enemy of kingdom authority as it lulled him (today it could be you or I) into a stalwart of comfort and convenience.

The fourth teachable moment of the third servant was laid out in the parable. It is an expectation of productivity and profitableness. As Jesus shared in the parable in Matthew 25:29-30, *[29]For to everyone who has, more will be given, and he will have abundance; but from him who does not have, even what he has will be taken away. [30]And cast the unprofitable servant into the outer darkness. There will be weeping and gnashing of teeth.*

As Kingdom citizens, God expects us to follow the model of His son Jesus Christ and engage in added value, reciprocity, and reproduction everywhere and at all times. We become an example of Jesus Christ when we become intentional about our Kingdom assignments and the word and the will of God for our lives.

I want us to take a moment to go a little further into this by examining these truths I've discovered about intentionality.

Truth #1
You have to be intentionally committed and committed to be intentional.

Truth #2
You can intentionally practice holding your life in a certain pattern.

Truth #3
Some people don't see the results they desire because they are not committed to the process of intentionality that leads to the desire end results.

Truth #4
Even though you may be currently "maintaining" you must still be intentionally focused on where you are going.

Truth#5
You have to have an intentional plan for an intentional life!

Please take a moment to write down a few truths that spoke to you about the power and necessity of being intentional.

TRUTH #1 _____

_____

_____

_____

_____

TRUTH #2 _____

_____

_____

_____

_____

TRUTH #3 _____

_____

_____

_____

_____

If you are going to move from a maintenance mindset and enter into the realm of intentional living, there is not any time for delay. Right now you must repent – change your mind – about the ways in which you may have been preoccupied and/or overly concerned about maintaining the status quo or things as usual and embrace the truth found in the word of God concerning His intentional plan for your life. Today, my prayer is that as we serve an intentional God we will become an intentional people who desire to do all we can to be "fruitful, multiply, subdue, and have dominion over all the earth."

LIFE AFFIRMATIONS

❖ I am no longer in maintenance mode. I purpose to live my life intentionally; just as God is intentional.

❖ I am loved by an intentional God who created me intentionally. I know He Has great plans for me.

❖ I pursue God's will for my life not haphazardly but with intention.

❖ I was created to be fruitful, subdue and have dominion on the Earth.

CHAPTER 1: NOTES

PERSONAL REFLECTION

CHAPTER 2

THE BIRTHING PROCESS
Trauma, Travail and Triumph

Ecc 3:1-2 "To everything there is a season. A time for every purpose under heaven. A time to be born...."

We understand there is a time to be born. In this chapter, I would like to address something else that should be understood. Before there is a time to be born there is a time to be processed and to be set up for birthing. We go through a certain season that prepares us to be born. The season and the process is for a set time to set us up for birthing. Yet, it is also a time for maturity. It is in that place of maturity we begin to grow and develop. We are here to birth God's reality into the Earth. When the will of God is agreed upon, produced and manifested in the Earth; it is called a Kingdom Reality. The Kingdom of God is now a reality in the Earth. I have penned this as our "TRIUMPH"! So let us deal with the process of birthing our TRIUMPH!

I've lived long enough to know that before every triumph of life, *nine times out of ten*, there has also been some trauma and travail. In this lesson, we will methodically walk through the process of Trauma, Travail, and Triumph using one of the most painfully riveting yet thought provoking stories of the Old Testament: the story of the "gift of God" herself – Hannah.

We will explore the following questions:

1. *What do you do when the pain of the promise seems to outweigh the purpose of the promise?*

2. *How do you agree with God when everything in your circumstances seems to be in disagreement with the word decreed?*

3. How do you prevail when the pain of the trauma and travail seem to outweigh the potential triumph?

HANNAH – GIFT FROM GOD

Have you ever experienced a time in your life when everything you experienced was the exact opposite of what you believed? Although it took me a while to get this, I've learned that there are some seasons in our lives where we will experience both intentional as well as unintentional trauma designed to abort the purpose and destiny of our lives. Let us examine this using the story of Hannah. In 1 Samuel 1:2, 9-18, we encounter a sweet woman with a loving husband who has everything except for the genuine desire of her heart – a son. It's ironic that Hannah, which means "gift from God", is unable to manifest a "gift from God" through her womb because of her seeming barrenness.

> **There are seasons in our lives where we will experience both intentional as well as unintentional trauma.**

Let's think about that for a moment. Here you are – a gift from God – but all of your prayers for God to bless your womb with a gift (male son) are not manifesting. Adding insult to injury is the fact that your husband's other wife has conceived time and time again. And just when you think this thing can't get worst, your Pastor accuses you of being drunk with wine!

1 Samuel 1:2, 9-18,
²And he had two wives: the name of one was Hannah, and the name of the other Peninnah. Peninnah had children, but Hannah had no children........ ⁹So Hannah arose after they had finished eating and drinking in Shiloh. Now Eli the priest was sitting on the seat by the doorpost of the tabernacle of the Lord. ¹⁰And she was in bitterness of soul, and prayed to the Lord and wept in anguish. ¹¹Then she made a vow and said, "O Lord of hosts, if You will indeed look on the affliction of Your maidservant and remember me, and not forget Your maidservant, but will give Your maidservant a male child, then I will give him to the Lord all

the days of his life, and no razor shall come upon his head." ¹²And it happened, as she continued praying before the Lord, that Eli watched her mouth. ¹³Now Hannah spoke in her heart; only her lips moved, but her voice was not heard. Therefore Eli thought she was drunk. ¹⁴So Eli said to her, "How long will you be drunk? Put your wine away from you!" ¹⁵But Hannah answered and said, "No, my lord, I am a woman of sorrowful spirit. I have drunk neither wine nor intoxicating drink, but have poured out my soul before the Lord. ¹⁶"Do not consider your maidservant a wicked woman, for out of the abundance of my complaint and grief I have spoken until now." ¹⁷Then Eli answered and said, "Go in peace and the God of Israel grant your petition which you have asked of Him." ¹⁸And she said, "Let your maid servant find favor in your sight. "So the woman went her way and ate, and her face was no longer sad.

The series of events were so traumatizing to Hannah that it could have robbed her of her God ordained promise and Kingdom purpose.

TRAUMA!

TRAUMA is defined as a deeply distressing or disturbing experience. Trauma can be an emotional shock following a stressful event or a physical injury often times associated with shock that can even lead to long term neurosis. Trauma can also be an emotional wound or shock that creates substantial and lasting damage to one's psychological development.

Hannah experienced some trauma in 1 Samuel 1:2, 9-8. First, she dealt with the trauma of being barren. Secondly, she dealt with the trauma of being ridiculed by her nemesis Peninnah who bore children. Finally, she dealt with the trauma of being accused of being drunk by her priest Eli. Let's look at it again. In 1 Samuel 1:2, it states, "And he had two wives: the name of one was Hannah, and the name of the other Peninnah. Peninnah had children, but Hannah had no children." We are

> **Trauma can be an emotional wound or shock that creates substantial and lasting damage to one's psychological development.**

very clear on Hannah's trauma. Let's explore how trauma has personally affected us. What trauma have you and I experienced that has been designed to hijack our purpose and destiny? To be clear, trauma can be something that can happen suddenly without warning that can severely shake and disturb your entire life. The scary thing about it is many people never recover from trauma in life!

In the case of Hannah, she is without a child and is being severely traumatized and provoked by Peninnah. While we know Hannah's heart is in pain because of the lack of fruitfulness in her life, I am convinced that the unrelenting absence of sympathy and antagonizing of Peninnah is what is really trying to get Hannah - a gift from God - to see herself as less than, useless, or worthless, anything but a gift from God. Let's dive a little deeper into it. If we are going to properly and effectively set ourselves free from the bondages of trauma, we must be aware of the fact that the enemy uses trauma – even those closest to us - to legally enter into your life to cause fear, bitterness and paralysis in all areas of life! In other words, one moment of trauma can shut down a lifetime of purpose!

> **If we are going to properly and effectively set ourselves free from the bondages of trauma, we must be aware that the enemy uses trauma to legally enter our lives.**

Below are some things I want you to ponder as it relates to TRAUMA:

PONDER POINT # 1
Trauma can either paralyze you or propel you forward!

PONDER POINT # 2
We have to be careful that our identity is in Christ and not in the trauma! While many people can accurately and passionately tell people about their trauma; however, many can't accurately and passionately talk about their identity in Christ.

PONDER POINT #3
Some of us have to go through trauma because we will be sent out to minister to others who have been traumatized.

PONDER POINT #4
Trauma will either make us bitter or better!

PONDER POINT #5
It is up to us to decide if we will stay in trauma or travail to get to triumph.

In the space provided below, write down some of the trauma you've experienced.

Some TRAUMAS I have experienced are:

1)

2)

3)

4)

5)

I know it may have been difficult to go through the process of writing down your trauma. However, it is a necessary first step in being delivered from trauma. Just like Hannah, our trauma is designed to drive us to the place of travail.

TRAVAIL

Travail is an intense form of intercession in which you are pregnant with God's will for something and you push through (usually in the form of groaning) until you give birth in the spirit to victory. Another way to think about it is that travail gives birth to something that didn't previously exist. In other words, travail always gives birth to the NEW and it always gives birth to Kingdom Realities.

> **Travail is an intense form of intercession.**

Again, let's look at the pattern of trauma, travail, and triumph in Hannah's life. Hannah travails before the Lord to birth the prophet Samuel which will bring a NEW word in the earth that will not fall to the ground. To travail is no easy burden. Why? It is heart wrenching. Travail is painful. Travail is burdensome. 1 Samuel 1:20 says, *"So it came to pass in the process of time that Hannah conceived and bore a son, and called his name Samuel, saying, Because I have asked for him from the Lord."* In her travail, Hannah positioned herself for triumph. So much so that as it is written in 1 Samuel 2:7, *God opened up Hannah's womb and gave her many more children.*

THE DIFFERENCE

Hannah's travail made the difference. It turned the tables, it changed up the odds and it confused and defeated the enemy. While she was tempted to just throw in the towel and quit; through anguish and tears mixed with heart wrenching prayers to our almighty God, Hannah's travail grabbed God's attention. I've learned that there are times in this life that we have to cry out to

God so deeply that we don't care what others say because they don't have our breakthrough or victory in the hands.

Let me ask you these questions? When was the last time you cried out in travail to God for your next level of breakthrough? When was the last time you got on your face and asked the Lord to move beyond natural circumstances and do the supernatural in your life? When was the last time you said, "If I perish, I perish but Lord don't leave me this way?" When was the last time you triumphed through your travail?

Now that I have you thinking, let me share what TRAVAIL means to me:

T – TRUST in God.

R – RESIST the urge to quit.

A – ADVANCE to the next level.

V – VEER- Change your perception and projectory through prayer.

A – AVAIL to God's leading.

I – IGNITE a passion to pursue God's will.

L– LIVE and never stop believing.

The most powerful thing in our travail is that we are NOT alone. During these times, the Lord our God fights our battles. Jesus Christ our elder brother stands in the gap for us, and the Holy Spirit gives us comfort, peace, and joy!

As we stand firm in travail, we are assured of this one thing, in the end, we win! As it is written in John 16:20-21 "*[20]I assure you, most solemnly I tell you, that you shall weep and grieve, but the world will rejoice. You will be sorrowful, but your sorrow will be turned into joy. [21]A woman, when she gives birth to a child, has grief anguish, agony because her time has come. But when she has delivered the child, she no longer remembers her pain trouble, anguish because she is so glad that a man a child, a human being has been born into the world."* It is in our travail that we are given a divine opportunity to birth a holy thing. Yet we must first press past the natural circumstances designed to hinder, misalign, and abort our destiny.

MARY'S HOLY THING

In the Kingdom of God, everyone has a process divinely orchestrated by God to get us from our "going through" of trauma and travail to our triumph in Jesus Christ. Often times, however, our "to" process of triumph is prematurely snuff out by the pains and pressures of life as the enemy tricks us into believing that the process is "unto death." In reality, however, we know that our process is for a set time, it is for a season, and most importantly the trauma and travail of our process is to birth new life in and through us.

> **In the Kingdom of God, everyone has a process divinely orchestrated by God.**

Let's dig a little deeper by reexamining the familiar story of Mary. *26 Now in the sixth month [of Elizabeth's pregnancy] the angel Gabriel was sent from God to a city in Galilee called Nazareth, 27 to a virgin [a]betrothed to a man whose name was Joseph, a descendant of the house of David; and the virgin's name was Mary. 28 And coming to her, the angel said, "Greetings, favored one! The Lord is with you." 29 But she was greatly perplexed at what he said, and kept carefully considering what kind of greeting this was. 30 The angel said to her, "Do not be afraid, Mary, for you have found favor with God. 31 Listen carefully: you will conceive in your womb and give birth to a son, and you shall name Him Jesus. 32 He will be great and eminent and will be called the Son of the Most High; and the Lord God will give Him the throne of His father David; 33 and He will reign over the house of Jacob (Israel) forever, and of His kingdom there shall be no end." 34 Mary said to the angel, "How will this be, since I am a virgin and have no intimacy with any man?" 35 Then the angel replied to her, "The Holy Spirit will come upon you, and the power of the Most High will overshadow you [like a cloud]; for that reason the holy (pure, sinless) Child shall be called the Son of God. 36 And listen, even your relative Elizabeth has also conceived a son in her old age; and she who was called barren is now in her sixth month. 37 For with*

God nothing [is or ever] shall be impossible." ³⁸ Then Mary said, "⁽ᵇ⁾Behold, I am the servant of the Lord; may it be done to me according to your word." And the angel left her.
—Luke 1:26-38

Mary agreed with God to conceive a Holy Thing within her and to birth a Holy Thing. In between the conception of the Holy Thing and the birthing of the Holy Thing; Mary had to endure the process that forms and prepares the Holy Thing for birthing. She experienced trauma in that the circumstances surrounding the birth of her Holy Thing was intense.

Ultimately, she made a choice to embrace her divine process when she said, *"I am the handmaiden of the Lord; let it be done to me according to what you have said."* Mary's embrace of her process paved the way for her ability to conceive, as she believed the word of the Lord and not her trauma. Additionally, when we agree to conceive what God has said, our wombs not only come to life but other wombs are awakened with life. In the case of Mary, it was her cousin Elizabeth. As it is written in Luke 1:36-37, *"And listen! Your relative Elizabeth in her old age has also conceived a son, and this is now the sixth month with her who was called barren. For with God nothing is ever impossible and no word from God shall be without power or impossible of fulfillment."*

> **Mary's embrace of her process paved the way for her ability to conceive as she believed the word of the Lord and not her trauma.**

Some things to ponder and learn from Mary's story are:

PONDER POINT #6
Conception begins at the point of agreement.

PONDER POINT #7
In order to birth a Kingdom Reality, our constant travail must be "Lord your Kingdom come and your will be done in the earth as it is in heaven!"

PONDER POINT #8
A Kingdom Reality is when the will of God is agreed upon and is produced or manifested in the earth.

PONDER POINT #9
We are here to birth God's Reality unto the earth!

PONDER POINT #10
Our ability to birth God's Reality in the earth impacts the lives of those not yet born. People benefit when we catch the revelation!

PROPHETIC DECLARATION

Once you agree with God for His will to be done in you (the Earth) as it is in Heaven, the Holy Spirit will overshadow you, grant you favor, and manifest good success in your life!

TRIUMPH!

On the other side of trauma and travail is triumph. Yes, I said it! On the other side of your pain, embarrassment, rejection, ridicule and scorn is triumph. Triumph means to overcome, to gain victory, to have good success and it is promised to each and every one of us who endures through our process to get to our next level of development and promotion in Christ. Still, given the cyclical nature of life, successfully navigating through this life requires that we develop the skill set necessary to not get stuck and/or derailed in trauma when it attempts to rear its ugly head again!

I am convinced that if we are going to maintain our posture and position of triumph, we must be intentional in growth in three areas: SPIRITUAL, EMOTIONAL, and RELATIONAL. In the subtitle of his book, Emotionally

Healthy Spirituality, Peter Scazzero writes, "It is not possible to be spiritually mature while remaining emotionally immature." Therefore, the mandate is on us to do a self-inventory and evaluation of our lives in the areas that were left open as a result of unresolved issues and trauma.

I just want to take a moment to strongly encourage you to take some time and write in the space below the areas wherein you need God to reveal and heal the trauma in your life.

_____

_____

_____

_____

_____

_____

_____

_____

Also, I would like to offer you the following prescription that has brought healing and wholeness into my own life in the area of trauma.

Pastor Law's Triumph Prescription

1. A Daily Dose of Remembering Who You Are In Christ – Say, "I am more than a conqueror through Jesus Christ!

2. A Reevaluation of Your Salvation – Knowing that you are saved by grace – God's unmerited favor – and loved by God!

3. A Reaffirmation of Your Faith – Remind Yourself of the Truth of God found in the Word of God.

LIFE AFFIRMATIONS

❖ I agree with God's plan for my life and I will not abort the process.

❖ Like Hannah, I will travail until I birth the promise God has for me.

❖ I will not allow the traumatic experiences in my life to make me bitter. I will allow God to work through me in those experiences to make me better.

❖ I recognize that my trauma is a tool to minister to others that have had similar traumatic experiences.

CHAPTER 2: NOTES

PERSONAL REFLECTION

CHAPTER 3

OVERCOMING THE JEZEBEL SPIRIT

In the last chapter we talked about trauma. Trauma can be any type of "deeply distressing or disturbing experience." If you are alive right now, guess what? You have either gone through trauma or are about to go through trauma. Now listen to me clearly, as a Pastor, I understand the importance of edification and exhortation. At the same time, however, I also understand the importance and power of equipping the saints. Additionally, if we are going to be properly positioned as well as equipped to go out and make disciples, we must be healed, delivered, and set free from all the physical, emotional, and psychological traumas that seek to rob us of our righteousness in Christ.

I truly believe that one of the greatest traumas currently harassing and robbing the body of Christ is the "deeply distressing and disturbing experiences" that come through the disconnection and disjunction in the family. Now you may be wondering, what does this have to do with overcoming the Jezebel spirit? In this chapter, we will explore the following:

1. What is the Jezebel spirit?
2. How has this spirit infiltrated the family?
3. What are some of the signs of the Jezebel spirit?
4. How to overcome this spirit and bring healing and wholeness to your family?

FREEDOM

The Lord has revealed to me some of the hindrances and attacks that were hiding in the darkness, which has limited, and slowed down the ability of my church and ministry to walk in the fullness of freedom. Whether it was a shift in service midstream or downloads I received to share via Periscope and other social media platforms, I am 100% convinced of what the Lord shared with me about overcoming the Jezebel spirit.

Moreover, I know that freedom is going to hit the church like never before as powerful things are already happening. If you will take this lesson as a "heads up" and blueprint to help you navigate those areas of your life that had been ripe for the infiltration of that foul spirit.

> **Freedom is going to hit the church like never before as powerful things are already happening.**

PRAY WITH ME

Father, in the name of Jesus, we thank you now for the revelation and education that will come through this lesson. Father, I decree and declare a special blessing of peace and protection upon all reading and teaching this lesson. We bind retaliatory spirits, spirits of doom, doubt, and depression. Father we call on Jehovah Rophi, God Our Healer to go before us now and remove every obstacle, stumbling block, spirit, and even physical being that would seek to harm, hurt, or hinder our freedom and liberty in you. Father we decree and declare whom the Son sets free is free indeed and today we release ourselves spirit, soul, and mind from the Jezebel spirit and attach our whole being to you and the truth of your healing word not by power, not by might but by your spirit, says the Lord. In Jesus name, Amen!

TWO BECOME ONE

I believe one of the greatest gifts God has ever given man is the covenant of marriage. And while we understand that both family and marriage is under attack as a result of cultural and legal decisions, I still believe the covenant of marriage is one of the greatest institutions of the Kingdom of God. Let's look at what Jesus said about the institution of marriage. In Matthew 9: 4-6 it reads, He replied, "*⁴Have you never read that He who created them from the beginning made them male and female, ⁵ and said, 'For this reason a man shall leave his father and mother and shall be joined inseparably to his wife, and the two shall become one flesh'?* ⁶ *So they are no longer two, but one flesh."*

Wow! Did you read that? So they are no longer two, but one flesh. The question, however, is what happens to the covenant and institution of marriage when the Jezebel spirit enters in and refuses to see the "two as one flesh" because the parental figure(s) have never released that son or daughter to leave and cleave? *As a matter of fact, the Jezebel spirit has entered in and become stronger than governmental and societal rulings on things such as same sex marriage. You may have a family member of your spouse; bartering, bruising and emotionally, psychologically and spiritually abusing you because that is their baby and they are not ready to let go.*

> **One of the greatest gifts God has ever given man is the covenant of marriage.**

THE ATTACK AGAINST MARRIAGE

As the Lord began to download in my spirit and reveal to me how many of us in the body of Christ were almost missing it. It still blows my mind at just how subtly the Jezebel spirit infiltrates our households and our marriages while the things of this world distract us. The scary thing about the Jezebel Spirit is you may not even realize it is happening under your nose. Let me be very clear because while I may not be teaching to everyone in this lesson; I know three things about the attacks on marriage through the infiltration of the Jezebel spirit:

- ❖ Either you are going through this attack
- ❖ You are coming out of this attack
- ❖ You have come out of this attack.

In particular, one of the ways that the Jezebel spirit is attacking marriages in the body of Christ is through the family's attachment to the husband and wife who are now one. Let me break it down for you. One of the ways that the

Jezebel spirit comes is through mothers. Sometimes it is the mother of the husband in the marriage. The manipulation and control going on is to divide the marriage and hurt the marriage both knowingly and unknowingly.

Unfortunately, what I've seen happen is that many mothers are engaging in fouls on the play as well as intercepting the ability for their sons to "leave and cleave" by interjecting their thoughts and opinions about the wife, competing both subtly and overtly for attention, affection, and gifts at the expense of their son's wife. They are doing too much which causes both division and strife within the son's house and with his wife.

> **The Jezebel Spirit subtly infiltrates our households and our marriages, while the things of this world distract us.**

The root cause of this attack can stem from the desire and need of the mother to:

- ❖ Manipulate and control
- ❖ Harbor unmet or unrealistic expectations
- ❖ Cling to past expectations
- ❖ Hold on to unfulfilled dreams and goals
- ❖ Refuse to respect boundaries
- ❖ Be the top priority
- ❖ Living life through their adult children

The end result of a mother's refusal to reposition herself out of her offspring's marriage is that it inevitably opens the door for an attack of the Jezebel spirit that can destroy the union.

What is the Jezebel Spirit?

The Jezebel spirit is a spirit of witch craft that uses control, manipulation, the power of innuendo and suggestion, deceit, flattery, attention, revenge, and "what about me" to position people and situations for its desired outcomes and expectations. In marriages, the Jezebel spirit is coming through in-laws and family members. In particular, it comes through people who are bitter, through people who refuse to respect boundaries, and through people who are insecure. At times, these people say "I wouldn't have chosen them for you or I never liked them anyway." In a nutshell, the attack through the Jezebel spirit is coming through people who are very envious of your marriage and speak all manners of evil against "what God has put together". They operate in blind lust and envy. They have ignored or forgotten the second part of the verse, which reads "let no man tear asunder" (Mark 10:9).

> **The Jezebel Spirit is a spirit of witchcraft that uses control and manipulation to position people and situations for its desired outcomes and expectations.**

Some of the ways you see or experience the Jezebel spirit in operation to attack and destroy marriages are as follows:

1. It seeks to give bad advice or counsel.
2. It doesn't say the same thing to both spouses (divide and conquer).
3. It meddles and or gives unsolicited opinions.
4. It talks about and gossips about the spouse with others.
5. It shares confidential and personal information.
6. It fellowships with those who do not like the spouse.
7. It keeps in contact with ex-spouses, partners, boyfriends, or girlfriends.
8. It always has to be the center of attention at family gatherings.
9. It always finds flaws or faults with the spouse being attacked.
10. It always tries to divide the children against the spouse.
11. The behavior does not manifest or reflect the fruit of the spirit and is evil in word, deed, and action as its end goal is to divide and break the marriage apart.

Please hear me very clearly; while we would be deceived into believing that the enemy is attacking the covenant of marriage solely through same sex relationships; the enemy is attacking marriages through those who struggle to release their sons to be the husband to the woman he loves.

The end result of the rise of the Jezebel spirit in marriages is constant interference. There is a lack of respect for boundaries. There is division within the marriage unit wherein the son is in the middle volleying between the manipulation, control, and subtle innuendo of the mother and his love for his wife.

Can we be honest? I know this might be a little uncomfortable for some of you all reading and teaching this lesson so I will use myself as an example. Growing up, my mother did two things exceptionally well. The first thing she taught me was how to be a good and respectable son. The second thing she did was to raise me to be a good husband. In raising me to be a good husband we have to assume that my mother sowed some fruit in me that she hoped would produce from a marriage harvest that maybe she didn't experience. In raising me not just to be a son but to also be a good husband and occupy other positions in life. What if my mother forgot to or had a hard time releasing me to be all that I am called to be for my beautiful wife LaWanda?

Flow with me! What if while raising me and watching me become a worthy son and admirable husband, my mother somewhere along the line, unknowing attached her hopes, dreams, and ambitions to me? What if secretly and innocently my mother vowed that there would never be a woman who could "love me as much and as good as she could"? Lastly, what if the entire time the enemy was lurking around waiting for the appointed time to make good on the secret thoughts of a woman - whom I also loved?

Let's SELAH on the truth of just how foul, corrupt, and dangerous this spirit is not just on the institution of marriage but also on the mothers and in-laws around the world being held captive and tormented by it.

OVERCOME WITH BOUNDARIES

While both my mother and my wife's mom individually and collectively went through their own processes and struggles of releasing my wife and I to "leave and cleave". I am Godly proud to share that my wife and I have a phenomenal marriage that we love. How? We were able to accomplish this by setting boundaries.

In order to get to where we are today we had to set boundaries. Quite honestly it wasn't always easy but we had to do some work to overcome the Jezebel spirit even in our own household. I can't overemphasize the importance of establishing and communicating **BOUNDARIES**. I want you to think about boundaries as your firewalls of protection. A boundary is a line that marks the limit of an area. It creates a divine line, a do not pass go demarcation; a this is a "no-no" area of your life. In other words, boundaries are our personal cease and desist notices.

One of the most powerful things about boundaries is that they set order and protocol. If you are going to overcome the Jezebel spirit you have to set boundaries with your family. In essence, you are going to have to tell everyone that my marriage and my wife are off limits. You have to put everyone on notice that commentary, advice, and unsolicited opinions about your marriage are not welcomed or tolerated.

You may have to set boundaries around the following:

- ❖ Who can come to your home (especially during the first 2 years of marriage)
- ❖ What information is shared with others
- ❖ What behavior and language pertaining to your spouse is and is not acceptable

The most important thing is to establish and set boundaries based on your situation and the desired Kingdom results you believe God to manifest in your marriage and family unit.

PRAYER

The second thing you have to do is engage in prayer and be open to understanding (revelation) as the Holy Spirit reveals who, what, when, where, and root cause of the attack. You must engage in prayer to ask God for wisdom and direction so as not to strike the rock when God is saying speak to the rock. What am I getting at? There have been times that the spouse under attack by a mother or in-law grows frustrated and weary with the seeming silence of the spouse. In particular, when the Jezebel spirit is coming through the mother and the husband seems impotent to do anything, you must pray, as you may not be aware of the control, manipulation, and witchcraft that the mother has used against the son his entire life. More often than not, this spirit rises up because the mother sees the spouse as a threat to her way of life. Think about it ... What if the mother has "guilted" her way into getting a portion of the son's income his entire life? If you have been married two years and she has been controlling and manipulating him for 30 years; without prayer and a divine revelation from God, the mother's voice will always reign supreme.

Until a man speaks out of his place of authority, nothing will change. You must pray for a divine revelation of God, an infilling and infusion of the Holy Spirit, and denouncing of all unclean and evil spirits attached to your spouse, and an overcoming spirit to conquer and defeat this distracting spirit once and for all. As you gain revelation of what to do, when to do it, and perhaps even why to do it, you must be obedient and without delay in what the Lord is speaking.

Quite honestly, the Lord may ask you to do the following:
- ❖ Pray for the mother or in-law causing strife in your household
- ❖ Forgive the mother or in-law for what they have done and/or said

❖ Forgive your spouse for not walking in his or her place of authority and establishing proper boundaries

❖ Forgive yourself for any resentment, anger, bitterness, strife, and unforgiveness you have harbored

❖ Tell the truth about the nature of the relationship and speak and wash it in the word of God knowing that we have this ministry of reconciliation.

STAND IN THE TRUTH

Regardless of the weight and heaviness of the attack you may have experienced or may be experiencing through the Jezebel spirit, you just stand in and on the truth of the word of God that what He has put together "no man shall tear asunder." Let me make it plain. If you are going to overcome and put to death the Jezebel spirit in your marriage you MUST KNOW, BELIEVE, DECREE, AND DECLARE THE FOLLOWING:

1. MY MARRIAGE IS ORDAINED BY GOD!

2. MY MARRIAGE & MY FAMILY IS COVERED IN THE BLOOD OF JESUS & SEALED BY GOD!

3. THE ENEMY HAS NO PLACE IN MY MARRIAGE, FAMILY, AND HOUSEHOLD!

> **You must take heart in knowing that while you may have been the intended target of the attack. Ultimately God's word has been under attack.**

You must take heart in knowing that while you may have been the intended target of the attack, ultimately God's word has been under attack. As such, God will recompense and destroy this evil and vicious spirit that is trying to destroy one of his beloved institutions. Many that operate in the Jezebel spirit are blinded to the fact that it's not you that they are messing with and causing pain. They are messing with what God put together!

Let me say this to anyone reading this right now. If you have ever operated or are operating in the Jezebel spirit in someone's marriage or family, you are out of order. You need to REPENT RIGHT NOW! You must repent because you are violating spiritual laws. You are in enmity with God's concept not who your son or daughter married. Again, one of the ways God moves through the earth is through families. When someone tries to mess with the marriage through the spirit of Jezebel, witchcraft, or manipulation, it is a direct slap in God's face. If you have done anything to violate God's institution of marriage, again, REPENT RIGHT NOW because to mess with a marriage is trespassing. It is the equivalent of committing a felony. If you violate God's marriage covenant, there will be an indictment, a charge, and some consequences in your life as a result of your actions.

God is now exposing and breaking up the foul spirit of Jezebel because it is in violation of what he covenanted in Matthew 19:4-6. Moreover, just like God declared in Isaiah 61, he is also setting husbands and wives and marriages free!

Isaiah 61: 1-3 AMP

The Spirit of the Lord God is upon me,
Because the Lord has anointed and commissioned me
To bring good news to the humble and afflicted;
He has sent me to bind up [the wounds of] the brokenhearted,
To proclaim release [from confinement and condemnation] to the [physical and spiritual] captives
And freedom to prisoners,

To proclaim [a]the favorable year of the Lord,
[b]And the day of vengeance and retribution of our God,
To comfort all who mourn,

To grant to those who mourn in Zion the following:
To give them a [c]turban instead of dust [on their heads, a sign of mourning],

The oil of joy instead of mourning,
The garment [expressive] of praise instead of a disheartened spirit.
So they will be called the trees of righteousness [strong and magnificent,
distinguished for integrity, justice, and right standing with God],
The planting of the Lord, that He may be glorified.

LIFE AFFIRMATIONS

❖ I have the courage to establish boundaries with my family regarding my marriage.

❖ I am filled with God's wisdom concerning my marriage.

❖ I follow God's blueprint for my marriage. As a result, I leave my family and cleave to my spouse, because my spouse and I are one.

❖ I am open to divine revelation from God concerning my marriage. I give him permission to uncover any hidden residue from the Jezebel spirit that may be operating in my life.

❖ I am more than a conqueror and I have overcame and conquered the distracting spirit of Jezebel.

❖ I am willing and obedient to God's instructions and I implement them quickly; without fear or hesitation.

❖ I release from my mental prison any anger, resentment, bitterness, strife and unforgiveness I have towards my in-laws because of their ignorance. I forgive them for their hurtful actions and words towards me.

❖ I forgive my spouse for not walking in their place of authority and establishing proper boundaries.

❖ I repent for the times I have operated under the Jezebel spirit. I remain sensitive to the spirit of God and will not ignore the Holy Spirit warnings when I am in error.

CHAPTER 3: NOTES

PERSONAL REFLECTION

CHAPTER 4

THE POWER OF GRACE

If you are like me, I am sure there have been times in your life where you've thought to yourself, what is wrong with me? You know how it is when you go through a personal interrogation and a Job-like list of personal accomplishments.

Have you ever thought to yourself?

- I have done all the right things.
- I have my education.
- I have developed my skills.
- I have served others.
- I have a lot to offer.
- I even go to church.

Now you may have a list a little bit different than mine but you already know where I am going with this. In spite of our long lists of accolades and accomplishments, it still seems as if nothing has worked out for our good.

The fact that you feel as if you've worked hard to achieve success, you've worked hard to equip and empower others, and you've worked hard for God without favorable results or outcomes can be overwhelming. In a nutshell, the problem is that you feel as if your best is not enough. Have you noticed that a keyword in all of this is "feel?" The danger is if we don't harness and master what we "feel," we can miss the main ingredient in our next dimension of growth and development. I am convinced that the reason why so many of us are experiencing lack luster miracles, signs, and wonders is because

> **The danger is if we don't harness and master what we "feel", we can miss the main ingredient in our next dimension of growth and development.**

we have hindered and limited the supernatural and transformative power of the GRACE OF GOD.

THE G FACTOR

If you are "feeling" like there is more to this heavy rotation of life -work ...eat... worship... sleep ... - that many in the body of Christ are on, I humbly submit to you that the missing ingredient is God's grace. What is grace? The classic definition of grace is God's unmerited or underserved favor toward sinners. In 2 Peter 3:18 (AMP), it says, *"but grow [spiritually mature] in the grace and knowledge of our Lord and Savior Jesus Christ. To Him be glory (honor, majesty, splendor), both now and to the day of eternity."*

The power and beauty of God's grace is that it affords joy, pleasure, delight, sweetness, charm, loveliness, good-will, loving-kindness, favor and the merciful kindness of God. It is God exerting his holy influence upon souls to turn them to Christ. I believe one of the keys to achieving success in life is to prepare and grow in grace and in the knowledge of God. You cannot live before God randomly and expect random blessings. I want us to examine a familiar New Testament passage.

> **One of the keys of achieving success in life is to prepare and grow in grace and in the knowledge of God.**

In Luke 5:1-8, it reads:

"¹One day as Jesus was preaching on the shore of the Sea of Galilee,[a] great crowds pressed in on him to listen to the word of God. ² He noticed two empty boats at the water's edge, for the fishermen had left them and were washing their nets. ³ Stepping into one of the boats, Jesus asked Simon,[b] its owner, to push it out into the water. So he sat in the boat and taught the crowds from there. ⁴When he had finished speaking, he said to Simon, "Now go out where it is deeper, and let down your nets to catch some fish." ⁵ "Master," Simon replied, "we worked hard all last night and didn't catch a thing. But if you say so, I'll let the nets down again."⁶ And this time their nets were so full of fish they began to tear! ⁷ A shout for help brought their partners in the other boat, and soon both boats were filled with fish and on the verge of

sinking. ⁸ When Simon Peter realized what had happened, he fell to his knees before Jesus and said, "Oh, Lord, please leave me—I'm too much of a sinner to be around you."

So let's take a moment to look at some facts so that we can see the G factor in action.

FACT #1
The men in this passage of scripture were skilled fishermen.

FACT #2
The men in this passage of scripture knew what they were doing. In particular, they had the necessary knowledge to get the job done.

FACT #3
The men in this passage of scripture were hard workers. The scripture says, Simon replied, "We worked hard all last night and didn't catch a thing."

FACT #4
The men in this passage of scripture were doing all of the right things but did not have any results.

Did you see Fact #4? You have to catch that! They were doing ALL of the RIGHT things but did NOT have any RESULTS!!!

Currently, you may feel exactly like the men in this passage of scripture. You may look at your life and think, "I have been doing all the right things but have nothing to show for it."

If this is you, let me introduce fact #5.

FACT #5: The men in this passage of scripture experienced exponentially different results when the G factor - GRACE - came on the scene!!!! When the grace of God through Jesus entered in, Peter and the rest of the fishermen experienced **"EXCEEDINGLY ABOVE ALL THEY COULD ASK OR THINK!"**

When Jesus got on the boat with Simon, GRACE got on the boat!

Simply put, the life, power, and supernatural ability of Jesus got on the boat and overtook the natural abilities of the fishermen. Why? In the scripture, we see grace operating to produce a Kingdom harvest designed to teach Peter and the other fishermen that your ability fails in comparison to the supernatural ability of Jesus manifested through his favor.

In all you do, you must remember the following:

Your skills are not the problem. Perhaps the problem is your lack of growth, knowledge and understanding that comes through grace and prayer.

As Christians many of us have been toiling for years because we don't understand the Grace of God. Psalm 127:1 says, "Unless the Lord builds the house, they labor in vain who builds it; unless the Lord guards the city, the watchman stays awake in vain."

The church and the people of God have been laboring in vain for far too long! It's time for us to wake up to prayer and the Grace of God! I am just simply here to reintroduce you to the Grace of God.

God is calling us to grow in grace and knowledge of HIM! There is just too much of God's favor and goodness that we are not walking in and experiencing on a daily basis. Let's dig a little deeper into the G factor by examining these two passages of scriptures.

"For out of His fullness [the superabundance of His grace and truth] we have all received grace upon grace [spiritual blessing upon spiritual blessing, favor upon favor, and gift heaped upon gift]." John 1:16 (AMP)

[3] *"Blessed be the God and Father of our Lord Jesus Christ, who has blessed us with every spiritual blessing in the heavenly places in Christ,* [4] *just as He chose us in Him before the foundation of the world, that we should be holy and without blame before Him in love."*
- Ephesians 1:3-4 (NKJV)

We also must remember that God has given us everything we need to fulfill our purpose on the earth. In Genesis 1:26-28, God said, "Be fruitful and multiply; fill the Earth and subdue it, have dominion over every living thing."

Finally, we must remember that God loved us so much that he sent His son to die for you and me. John 3:16 reads, *"He did not send his son to condemn the world, but that the world through Him might be saved."* As you live your life according to your spiritual DNA, you will grow in grace and experience blessings and favor. God in His grace is calling and empowering you to grow in spiritual maturity and Christlikeness. Can you sense God in His graciousness, yearning to influence every area of your life? I am not speaking of an emotional feeling but rather a spiritual recognition of the wisdom, stature, and favor God has bestowed on us.

> **As you live your life according to your spiritual DNA, you will grow in grace and experience blessings and favor.**

HINDRANCES OF GRACE

Several things may be keeping you from living in the fullness of God's grace. It could be fear, doubt, apathy, religion, tradition, rebellion, disobedience or dishonor. However, catch this, I believe one of the unspoken hindrances of grace is **HONOR.** To honor is to esteem someone. It is to hold someone in high regard. It is to place their needs above our own. The problem sometimes is that we "honor" people with lip service but fail to do so with our actions and output. Let me give you an example. You can say you love someone yet never show them honor in how (actions & output) you love them.

Sometimes we fail to honor others because we have made them common or too familiar. The danger with the spirit of familiarity is that it will blind you and you won't be able to recognize the favor and grace of God when it comes to change your life.

In Matthew 13:54-58, we learn of the danger of familiarity in the life of Jesus. "*54 When He had come to His own country, He taught them in their synagogue, so that they were astonished and said, 'Where did this Man get this wisdom and these mighty works? 55 Is this not the carpenter's son? Is not His mother called Mary? And His brothers James, Joses,[a] Simon, and Judas? 56 And His sisters, are they not all with us? Where then did this Man get all these things?' 57 So they were offended at Him. But Jesus said to them, "A prophet is not without honor except in his own country and in his own house." 58 Now He did not do many mighty works there because of their unbelief."* The people knew and loved Jesus BUT THEY DID NOT HONOR HIM! As a result, they didn't receive Him and the fullness of His grace. The end result of the spirit of familiarity was that the people shut down their own breakthroughs!

Now, let's take a look at a group of people that recognize the gift that Jesus was and chose to honor him. In John 4:39-45 it states,
"*39 And many of the Samaritans of that city believed in Him because of the word of the woman who testified, "He told me all that I ever did." 40 So when the Samaritans had come to Him, they urged Him to stay with them; and He stayed there two days. 41 And many more believed because of His own word.42 Then they said to the woman, "Now we believe, not because of what you said, for we ourselves have heard Him and we know that this is indeed the Christ,[a] the Savior of the world."43 Now after the two days He departed from there and went to Galilee. 44 For Jesus Himself testified that a prophet has no honor in his own country. 45 So when He came to Galilee, the Galileans received Him, having seen all the things He did in Jerusalem at the feast; for they also had gone to the feast."*

> **The danger with the spirit of familiarity is that it will blind you and you won't be able to recognize the favor and grace of God when it comes to change your life.**

The end result is that the people received Jesus and were blessed and saved. They didn't dishonor the gift and cut off the grace on their lives!

BUT GOD...

> *"¹And you He made alive, who were dead in trespasses and sins, ² in which you once walked according to the course of this world, according to the prince of the power of the air, the spirit who now works in the sons of disobedience, ³ among whom also we all once conducted ourselves in the lusts of our flesh, fulfilling the desires of the flesh and of the mind, and were by nature children of wrath, just as the others.⁴ **But God**, who is rich in mercy, because of His great love with which He loved us, ⁵ even when we were dead in trespasses, made us alive together with Christ (by grace you have been saved), ⁶ and raised us up together, and made us sit together in the heavenly places in Christ Jesus, ⁷ that in the ages to come He might show the exceeding riches of His grace in His kindness toward us in Christ Jesus.* -Ephesians 2: 1-7

I want to add a new definition of grace. My new definition of grace is *BUT GOD!* I believe "*BUT GOD*" are two of the most powerful words in the Bible. Regardless of what is going on in our lives; no matter what we have been guilty of *BUT GOD* has cleansed us, made us the righteousness of Christ, and adopted as sons. We were dead in trespasses and sins; disobedience, lustful and rebellion *BUT GOD* granted us mercy and compassion.

Truth be told, we were slated for destruction and doomed but Christ was born to manifest a *BUT GOD* in our lives. The birth of Christ was His light coming into our lives to interrupt our darkness. Moreover, the gift of grace is His light shining down into the dark abyss of life and ushering in a *BUT GOD!* Grace comes in to change your life, turn it around and place you in righteousness. Regardless of your past, God can use you greatly if you choose to believe and trust in His grace.

The life of the Apostle Paul is a perfect example of God's grace. In I Corinthians 15:9-10, Paul writes, "*For I am the least of the apostles, who am not worthy to be called an apostle, because I persecuted the church of God. But by grace of God I am what I am, and His grace toward me was not in vain; but I labored more abundantly than they all, yet not I, but the grace of God which was with me.*" Catch this! Paul says he was the least of the apostles because of his past. At one time, Paul was an enemy of God and persecuted the Church of God. Through His grace, Paul was saved. Simply put, Paul had a *BUT GOD* experience! Don't allow the Grace of God on your life to be in vain and of no effect. God has given you His Grace to live out His will for your life and accomplish everything He told you to do. Look at what Paul wrote in 1 Corinthians 15:10, "But by the grace of God I am what I am: and his grace which *was bestowed* upon me was not in vain; but I labored more abundantly than they all: yet not I, but the grace of God which was with me."

FIVE THINGS ABOUT GRACE

First, God's grace comes as a master to His inferiors. He gives grace to those who are inferior to him to bring them to a place where they no longer feel inferior. Secondly, grace comes to elevate your life. In essence, grace is God's kindness and gentleness towards us. Thirdly, we must always remember that Jesus brought grace to the earth. Yet, the birth of Jesus was a blessing and a threat.

"[18] Now the birth of Jesus Christ was as follows: After His mother Mary was betrothed to Joseph, before they came together, she was found with child of the Holy Spirit. [19] Then Joseph her husband, being a just man, and not wanting to make her a public example, was minded to put her away secretly. [20] But while he thought about these things, behold, an angel of the Lord appeared to him in a dream, saying, "Joseph, son of David, do not be afraid to take to you Mary your wife, for that which is conceived in her is of the Holy Spirit. [21] And she will bring forth a Son, and you shall call His name Jesus, for He will save His people from their sins."[22] So all this was done that it might be fulfilled which was spoken by the Lord through the prophet, saying: [23] "Behold, the virgin shall be with child, and bear a Son, and they shall call His name Immanuel," which is translated, "God with us."[24] Then Joseph, being aroused from sleep, did as the angel of the Lord commanded him and took to him his wife, [25] and did not know her till she had brought forth her firstborn Son.[a] And he called His name Jesus."-Matthew 1:18-25

The fourth thing about grace is that just like Jesus, your birth is a blessing and a threat at the same time. Nothing about Jesus' birth made sense. The same may be true with you. If your birth did not make sense, was peculiar, and you find that people honor and dishonor you: please realize you are in good company. You are called to be peculiar; there is nothing normal about you. Finally, grace is not something you can earn. It is favor given to you while you are in an inferior place. Grace finds you at your worst. Personally, I want to be in covenant with those that understand grace. These are the people I will find Christ dwells in because they won't always point out my flaws. The law points out flaws while grace points out our strengths as identified through *BUT GOD* grace and favor.

OUR CHALLENGE

Every day when we wake up, we find Him right there by us and in us. For that reason alone, we should give God praise and gratitude for his grace. Take a moment and think about all the stuff you have been through and were not supposed to come through. How in the world do you think you got through it? You already know it is *BUT GOD* GRACE! Also, we must recognize that the grace of God is not an "IT"! Grace is actually the life, power, and ability of God through Jesus Christ on our lives. Another way to think about it is that grace is Jesus Himself manifesting in your life to do through you what you can't possibly do through yourself.

Remember these three truths about the *BUT GOD* grace we experience.

- ❖ The grace of God is the ability of God to live a life deeply planted and rooted in the principles and purposes of God!

- ❖ The Grace of God is also the wisdom, knowledge, and understanding of God in our lives to fulfill the will of God for our lives!

- ❖ God accomplishes His will for our lives by freely giving us the Grace of God to do it

LIFE AFFIRMATIONS

- ❖ God has cleansed me, made me the righteousness of Christ and I am adopted as a son/daughter of God.

- ❖ I recognize I will become successful in fulfilling my purpose and reaching my destiny by understanding God's grace.

- ❖ I recognize spiritually the wisdom, grace and favor God has given me.

- ❖ I purpose to increase my prayer life so that I flow with the grace of God.

- ❖ I honor those that God has given me as my spiritual leaders.

- ❖ I refuse to become too common and too familiar with my leaders that it causes me to operate in dishonor.

- ❖ I will not fail to receive my breakthrough because of a lack of honor.

- ❖ I am not bound to my past because Christ has shined His light on my darkness and I am created anew. My slate has been wiped clean and I have a fresh start in the Kingdom of God.

- ❖ The grace of God will not be in vain and of no effect in my life. I receive His forgiveness and grace.

- ❖ I have God's grace to fulfill His plans for my life.

- ❖ I am no longer inferior, but I am a joint heir with Christ. He is seated in heavenly places and I am seated right next to him.

- ❖ I embrace my call to be peculiar; a member of a royal priesthood.

- ❖ Like Christ, I won't magnify my flaws, but amplify my strengths.

- ❖ I know without a shadow of a doubt God's Grace is not an "it or thing", but it is LIFE, power and the ability of God through Jesus. I receive this GRACE.

- ❖ It is not in my strength but by the power of Jesus operating through me to love life deeply rooted in the principles of God.

CHAPTER 4: NOTES

PERSONAL REFLECTION

PRAYER OF SALVATION

Dear Lord, this is new for me. I'm not sure how to do this but I'm going to do my best. Today I ask for the courage and the faith to believe that You will save me and heal me. My life hasn't been the prettiest! I've made some mistakes. I'm asking for You to come into my life and beautify me! I've heard so much about Your love! I'm asking that you would fill my heart with Your love and Your joy! I've been told that Your Son died for me and my sins! I'm asking that Your Son Jesus Christ would come into my life and give me the relationship that I've always wanted! Please forgive me for delaying this moment and this decision for so long. But today I have the faith and the courage to believe that I definitely want Jesus Christ in my life as my Savior, my King and my Friend! I want to be more than saved! I want to be loved! Teach me this day how to receive Your love and how to share Your love! Today I make a decision to be a part of a new and loving family! I no longer have anything to fear! I know that you love me because today I believe in my heart and confess with my mouth and I make a decision to call you Lord! Thank you for forgiving me! Thank you for healing me! Thank you for restoring me! Thank you for loving me!

Thank you for saving me and calling me your own! Thank you for giving me the courage and the faith to make the right decision today! Lord Jesus, I don't know everything about You yet and I don't know all the Scriptures. But what I do know is that You love me and my life will never be the same again!

I love you Father! I love you Jesus!

Thank you again! Time to live now because *LIVING IS FOR EVERYONE* including ME!
Amen

ABOUT THE AUTHOR

Pastor Kenneth Karl Law is the Senior Pastor of a growing congregation located in Pooler, GA. He is an Inspiring Speaker, Advisor/Confidant to Pastors, Founder of LAW School for Leadership Development and a Spiritual Father to many; young and old. Pastor Law is a man with a true servant's heart and a man of great belief in covenant relationships. He served faithfully in ministry under the direction of his Spiritual Father, Bishop Eddie L. Long of New Birth Missionary Baptist Church in Lithonia, GA. After years of service as a member and as a Minister under Bishop Long, Pastor Law accepted his call to Pastor in August of 2007. He and his lovely wife (LaWanda) transitioned to Savannah to begin their journey as a satellite church under the New Birth umbrella in September of 2007. He also holds a Master's Degree in Theology.

Pastor Law teaches in a practical way that makes his messages very relatable and empowering to those under the sound of his voice. He has been blessed with a gift to tap directly into the heart of God so that you want to accept the invitation to come to Christ and you want to change your life to live by the principles set forth in God's word.

Pastor Law's Kingdom Agenda is to Love and Serve the People, Win Souls, Make Disciples and Advance The Kingdom of God. He has a passion for teaching Leadership and has a special anointing to empower other Pastors to continue strong in the journey. Through the ministry that lies within him, many souls have been saved and lives transformed with a greater pull to draw closer to God. Pastor Law has an international anointing and has traveled globally to minister to the people of God.

Pastor Law and his wife, Elder LaWanda R. Law, have been happily married since 1998. They proudly treasure the many children that God has allowed them to be surrogate parents to as their own. They are clearly establishing a living legacy of hope by extending the love of Jesus Christ to all those that they meet. With the leading of the Holy Spirit, they both walk in a posture of humility and with an understanding of **"to whom much is given much is required"**.

www.ingramcontent.com/pod-product-compliance
Lightning Source LLC
LaVergne TN
LVHW061217060426
835507LV00016B/1976